Messages to Lelia

Messages to Lelia: Haiku, Short Poems, and Longer Poems

BILLY REED

Cover photo credit:

New Urban Media
and New Urban Web Design
Memphis, Tennessee
https://newurbanmedia.co

Used by permission

Pin-oak leaf clip art from
Florida Center for Instructional Technology (FCIT)
http://fcit.usf.edu/

Other poems by Billy Reed
appeared in a limited-edition
2014 chapbook titled
on the levee road

A Coldwater Springs publication
Memphis, Tennessee

Printed by CreateSpace
https://www.createspace.com/6970826

To
William Wallace Pearson
Sumner, Mississippi

Table of Contents

Acknowledgments

Thanks to many friends for their encouragement and endurance over all these years, especially those who "liked" or commented on my Facebook postings! Thanks for your time and attention!

I also owe a debt of thanks to Robert Thompson for his persistent guidance toward the organization and publication of this book.

To Jon Forbus for his editing skills, his friendship and consultation.

To Terry Starr for her editorial assistance, her teaching, and her encouragement.

To Kenny Morrell for his early encouragement.

To my beloved wife Susan for her love and encouragement over many years.

To the "Great Spirit" for allowing me to be a poet.

Many Thanks!

Foreword

When Billy Reed began to display his own haiku poetry to friends on the Internet I was astonished. My loquacious pal could never compress a conversational anecdote into a few thousand words. How could he fit a thought into seventeen syllables? On inspection of this collection:

> it is clear he has
> mastered the art of haiku
> and longer verse too

After knowing Billy Reed for more than a half-century I should not be surprised. His long life has been full of enough experiences to inspire hundreds of poems—or a lengthy memoir for that matter. He's a product of West Tennessee who went off to an Army assignment in Germany before he ever enrolled at the school once called Southwestern at Memphis. He played football for the Lynx. He then did a valuable apprenticeship in the Mississippi Delta before returning to Memphis where he encountered the satisfaction and stress of a business entrepreneur; where he knew the joys and suffered the sorrows of romance.

Oddly enough, a dose of heartbreak serves as good strong medicine, especially for those who dare to write about life. It shows up in Billy's verse. He writes:

> he was born broken
> twisted, incomplete grew then
> lovely in spirit

I don't think Billy was "born broken," but some events in his life threatened to break him. I believe he managed to emerge from them still "lovely in spirit." That spirit shows through in his verse.

It's touching that Billy dedicated this volume to Bill Pearson, our ninety-something friend from our years in the Mississippi Delta in the 1960s and far beyond. Though Bill Pearson and his wife Betty live in retirement in California near their daughter Erie and her family, he remains a role model for a Southern gentleman. In the turbulent period when the civil rights movement engulfed the Delta, the Pearsons stood out as beacons of fairness and civility and reason in a sea of angry, thoughtless whites resistant to any change. Bill is wise, and he may be the most voracious reader I've ever known. Fittingly, Billy Reed and Bill Pearson were among the earliest members of a venerable Memphis book club that limited its chairs to seven in order to maintain a single orderly conversation around a dinner table.

I felt privileged to be invited to join the club in 2005. But I have felt privileged to know Billy and Bill for much longer, and it's nice to see them linked again in his volume of verse.

Curtis Carter Wilkie

Haiku and Short Poems
Images composed of few lines

when i did listen
all those years and years turned real
your stair and your voice

black seal on the sand,
still, pitted, far from herd
i will grieve you home.

sunlight in my room.
illumination, erased
if I close my heart

at awakening
he was quietly joyous
two more hours to sleep

i dream of life in
my mother's womb suspended,
floating in her soul.

he was born broken,
twisted, incomplete grew then
lovely in spirit.

he sleeps angel sleep
still, at peace with darkness, stark
naked and alone.

she mediates
morning by morning, reading
the psalms, asking peace.

he chose to love me
gave himself away prepared
me to sing and dance

great spirit of the night
and morning, here I am kill
me
open my heart.

each time they touched
definitions of tenderness
became obsolete

there is a small bridge
where grandmother often stands
the war is over

we talked it out,
anger ebbing, listening,
trusting each other
when mom died, dad, who
could not speak, wept childlike and
climbed into her bed

i see silent black
marble names known and unknown
remember claudie

we discussed windows
and rooms, electricity,
matters of the spirit

he walked through the streets
reminiscent of a ghost ship
lost from the sea

violet beauty
commands the room and renders
absolute silence

he sleeps all alone
not near any human sound
sometimes a small cat

that I seek to keep you
gives an energy
my being
is embraced beyond the sky
her eyes are patient
and hold me
as if touching

hidden from the rain
we danced the afternoon
singing in delight
grandsons

there is an infant
seldom embraced
or tended
please
go to her now

a celebration
last night's full moon reappears
breath becomes quiet

she prayed for a hat
for her ears not to be cold
she soon slept again

she often awoke
in mysterious places
not knowing the trees
or faces of those nearby
once north of new orleans

on awakening
he could recognize no trees
thin men sweep the street

pink camellias
mistaken for butterflies
we meander home

a small man still sleeps
underneath his sister's porch
wisterias bloom

september sunlight
two small boys sip their chocolate
voices from upstairs

beneath the low bridge
asleep covered in kudzu
perhaps beyond sleep

his dog's grace
erases
with no words sung or spoken
yesterday's rain

he walked the desert
until it became bamboo
soon a baby cried
this august night
smells of cut grass and slow rain
mother sleeps on the porch

no one walks this path
she stands alone in the shade
breaths turn to prayer

across arkansas
a softly lit july moon
she walks in silence

she is lonely now
bird feeders all are empty
not even moonlight

rain softly comes down
from the porch swing she listens
can this be their train

he prefers his couch
shadows from a turning fan
few recollections
☐

Black dog on black stoop
Staring at small boy weeping
Through the wrought iron gate.

j.v. died three years ago,
exhausted and frail,
children at his side.
In the room unseen
A chorus of dancers came
Excited, expectant . . .

I long to embrace
the great spirit; be sustained
in her lush bosom

of his own hand
cleve died, consumed with madness,
aspiring to absence.

elgin saw angels
sitting in his swing, resting
from dancing all night.

no sun has risen
upon the dark edged delta
she walks in silence

what is the color
of mercy of compassion
i choose those colors!

anciently beautiful,
a long ago love came by--
we drank tea and talked;
communion

sometimes politeness
becomes lost in the thick weeds
of self-absorption.
a thinly curved moon
escaping from seclusion
not one sound is said

naked and tattooed
alone
breath comes difficult
he curls in a ball
back at boy scout camp
his name remains carved in wood
sisters search the entire night

her knitted brown hat
fallen from the beggar child
wet now and freezing

she would not cover her face
many men beat her
she stared straight at each

you took me away
you made me know calmness
to need to know none but you
to desire to be filled by only you

she was stark naked
standing on linoleum
listening for steps

accompany me
be the one who listens when
awkwardness prevails

of all the children
only one is standing still
she shrinks in sadness

climbed in now by boys
next to little bobby's grave
the tree mom planted

All night it rained ice
when light came trees were frozen
the outside was still
dogs refused to leave the house
electricity vanished

she
is bald from medication
still hopeful
waiting at the road's edge

dad became outraged at my disrespect;
mom protected me;
sister fled next door.

he thought back awhile
intimate again with grief
did she fly from here

she waits in darkness
leaf edges announce the sun
time to return home

you stand in willows
deep beyond the afternoon
I reach out for you

with a not clean skin
hair wound in oiling twistings
he hopes for coffee

faintly
over and over
she whispers
i am desperate for god

he heard them singing
as he walked past the windows
longed to be inside

will you come with me
put your cheek against my chest
hear my heart calling
please ask me to dance
let me be the one who twirls
who touches your hair

in october's sun
how I yearn for you
against my expectant face

lord i am small
i can barely speak or write
lend me your pencil

september sunlight
two small boys sip their chocolate
voices from upstairs
wrens weep all morning
smoke consumes ancient meadows
every sign says flee

these waterfalls sing
near to them dogs often dance
who notices rain

her bedside table
he touched worn beads of prayer
a sealed envelope

there is a not me
in this pose
or that
then
sometimes
along comes me

an old path seems odd
no men holding mules
no houses
no small bare feet

at the old house
a lawn like pasture grass
cars in the yard
ghosts waving
i love to lie here
to touch my beloved's back
to never know when
deep moments of sleep arrive
dreams of red dogs disappear

a silence prevails
yet sounds or music still breathe
then the small drummer

his rum glass empties
evening becomes uncertain
children hesitate

in the night rains came
every crevice clasps water
mothers chair floats still

she lost her slippers
alongside an ancient pond
sunlight soon returns

rain
came in the night
danced in
by dust filled field hands
too joyous to sleep
bare feet on the floor
shadow down the wall
gray light seeps across the room

she is beautiful
ancient as methuselah
filled with passion

waited in the desert
drawn there by sure perception
saw a tiny light

go to the desert
purify yourself waiting
dance with fierce and crude

broken heartedness
inconvenient as it is
is a precious thing

from poems by hafiz
all I know is love,
and I find my heart infinite
and everywhere

mysterious sounds
blindfolded football coaches
the basement is deep

a time of silence
egrets in the southern sky
two girls just stand there
she spoke of cats who
became at dusk men, comely
attentive and kind

what is the color
of mercy? of compassion?
i choose those colors!

please bury me
in a pinewood box—let earth
be custodian

it is difficult
to speak in the midst of
overwhelmimg sadness

shadow died at night
wounded and bleeding--unsaved
by grievous boy love

from the ancient lake
sounds seemed the same as when we
quietly lay there

a red haired woman
cannot find her way and weeps
in scared confusion

at morning prayer
a fierce resentment consumed
all adoration

when he departed
i climbed in his bed to feel
the remaining warmth

i saw martin king
walk through philadelphia
the crowd howled at him
fear was so strong
all saliva disappeared
from my tongue and my eyes

she resides in
phantasmagoria
silent seemingly alone

light from her heart
caused roaches to long for noon
bats to emerge at dawn

no poem manifests
silence reigns and ass stays screwed
tightly to his chair

she leaned from her car
and spat on the street then ate
a sack of cheetos

i lay
up in a hole
abandoned by myself
to become myself

now look at me
everywhere I am still
and silent

who sings
across the aisle
this man with shaking fingers
and tangled hair

susan
today is your birthday
for me it became
the day the earth moved

sometimes in winter
first light
makes leafless twigs sing out
notice me
now

you are precious
let me cheek touch yours
i want
to listen
to hear you

31

how many miles
is it to home
gray deep fog
be making me
lonesome

hard stilted moments
no compassion
little truth

she shivers
this odd girl
who has no coat
and speaks
only to herself

do you hold
your frightened child
hold me the same
sing me a song
rock me

in aunt zee's
bedside box
soiled telegrams
bourbon
dental tape
a knife

thank you
for things to clean
for energy
to haul the cleansing
waters

thanks
for the pain
in my knee
for life
that allows me to know the pain

she left here
darkness pervades
frost forms on every pain
my lips go numb

his prayer summoner
resentment
stood there
singing opportunity

awakened
not alone
recognizing no wall
or ceiling
she left

the pair of gloves
worn only once
hid among earmuffs
majorette boots

she said goodbye
just
not in those words
my lips tremble
in recognition

we all meander
amid the caves of hell
admiring the gardens
a familiar face
obscure
floating away
revives my longing

a tiny white bird
wounded in the side
almost not noticed

she was drunk
singing
in a mysterious tongue
slow dancing alone

two little girls
wait
near the place where buses stop
anxious for their mother

a remembered moon
and me
here at mother's tomb
the trees are larger

she was glad for gloves
her dad's pea jacket
an absence of wind

out my window
shadows
cross the darkening lake
like Cyprus trees
all fallen at once
floating

near the faded fence
odd mounds of twisted refuse
grown over by reeds
lovely blue wisteria
on april evenings a moon

this ground becomes as ice
strange snow hangs in every tree
the moon in cold shines
one girl in polka dot clothes
cannot see her clouded breath

one barren oak tree
along the curved levee road
unmoved by despair
confident of jonquil love
geese returning north to home

all day long it rained
disoriented cousins
came to remember

i come here with ancient love
and bring my every thought and dream
you beautiful girl torn by time
as the sea makes lovely the shore
rise and dance with me until day

last night she walked here
at the end of a day's work
soon she departed
determined
not in anger
her clothes being loosely packed

all my life I sought after you
not knowing if I would recognize
but this morning you seized me

can I see your face
or know you exist to touch
the answer comes no
yet you are my energy

the day winter ends
calendars make notation
but look at pear trees
such inspirations to bloom
in winter's final moment

rain in mist comes down
iced pathways become obscure
soon the earth trembles

at her eyes' one blink
gingko leaves restore the spring
these spare thin branches
yield to succulent greenness
what generous surrender

a long ago love
waiting near the wrought iron gate
greeting my children

the storm seems complete
then thin rivulets appear
inundation tells
how each empty place comes full
how high treetops disappear

in gray december
an eleven year old boy
stands by a bus stop
on the way to grandmother's
his back to northern wind

she hid in bamboo
no one found her secret place
he could weep alone

she lost her wine flask
it floated from the side porch
the third day of rain

scarlet tanagers
unseen since late september
took south all their figs

Longer Poems

Recollections

Three women walked a curved path.
Dresses dappled in rising light,
Morning shadows vanishing;
A sparsely populated caravan
Advancing through an ancient grove.
Moving, in their gravitational pull,
One eight year old boy.

The women speak of morning things and war,
The boy, anxious, listens.

And years later listens, when seething men
Congregate there, screaming their vile will
Through the stately trees at soldiers
And those now come to join.

And stands to the side,
Unable to speak for himself,
To say his truest heart,
Among those with whom he had grown.
Whose mothers held him
And grandfathers knew his name.

In the sunlit house

I walk to the sunlit house
Often she waits near the window
And looks to me with eyes of quiet longing

She then smiling touches my hand
And my face
I kneel to clasp her knees

She looks with more longing
And commands my embrace
In the midst of such love who could not call this perfection
We seek embrace
we give embrace

In my dream

In my dream I walked in low flat landscapes,
Crossing the nearly treeless fields alone.
Past dense greening corn and hedges on the pathways edge,
Through every aspect of every field I tramped.
Never did I thirst or fall exhausted.
My presence was strong as in younger days,
Not once have I dreamed myself as old.
Could dreams be cousins to the soul?
If so, this body that rises slowly from a chair,
These naked feet that totter along the night paths,
Can be not so beholden to dreams
But free to walk the soul's garden
And there to dance a dance of stillness
Unchanged since before the beginning.
Being conscious of neither youth or age but of light
Unchanged since before the beginning.

A river story

At dawn the river is still,
Yet full from rain, a curved moon wanes
The western shore; on the river road lights shine
then enter again the ancient forest,
Vast and silent, clasped to the river's bent edge.
Stand with me here and breathe the new morning!
See lines of geese now south bound
Lit by the soon gone moon and unseen sun,
Hear the geese sing above this silence,
Of frozen time, before the forest grew.
Hear again the silence as they fly
Beyond our senses; then hear the new,
As now again the ancient sounds come
In southbound sadness.

Here

This is not the end of all,
A last lonesome place.
There is another simple way,
Quiet with lesser light.
So, I beg you not fear fallen leaves,
Or weep in faded grass.
Near here there is a fair grove,
Grown fresh as ever bloomed.
It grows beside a worn path
Where winter comes as spring.
All along, bright flowers grow;
As birds sing in welcome song.
So, I ask you fair soul,
Onto this pathway come.

A friend

He sits at table, as do we all,
In straightback chair, quietly listening.
Yet his silence is not like the rest;
A sadness dampens the conversation.

Then we rise to leave, joshing as usual
And walk, talking, down a familiar stair,
I tug to his sleeve so he could follow;
Into the alleys and nearby avenue.

As we come into the street he hesitates
As if to speak to an assembled crowd.
His eyes lighting in anticipation,
Like ice lit when a winter moon comes clear.

No words follow; his lips move silently
While from his shaking throat
Comes enraged muteness,
As if it no longer knew of sound.
"already," I think, "he's reached the other side."

Dance

Beyond this small place where could I now exist
Better than here
An afternoon in the rooms of arriving friends
These bent chairs empty and waiting
Coffee pots against the wall
A boy in back turned cap
Sitting silent facing me.

It is not good to think
Beyond the fragrance of my cup of tea
Of calls waiting for return
Or yellow aspen leaves in flight.
All memory must be restrained;
Silence of my history celebrated.

So, outside this moment,
Essentials do not exist.
No woman, or child, or round of applause; no fresh caught fish;
No house with stained rounded windows; or club on the cape
With an ocean view porch.

What I need is here
The venetian blinds raised to the ceiling,
Coffee and cake laid on wood top tables,
Tissue boxes, bottles of water,
Oddly placed ceramic clocks,
Flower vases sometimes filled,
Each exotic and lonesome,
Seeking a dance from all who come here.

I beg your pardon as my eyes close and become quite still.
and listen to those who not so quietly arrive.
My being
Joins the dance now yet inside me.
No longer at the floor's edge
But in its heart among those who come
To be as one, dancing not alone, but
Midst all angels; transformed, dancing.

A message

Open your eyes
Breathe sublime breath

Open your eyes
Breathe sublime breath

When terrified ones seek to suck all air
When terrified ones seek all space
Say a prayer and give them a place
To whine or shine and die by shallow breaths

But you
Rejoice among impoverished ones
Breathe sublime breath
Open your eyes

at first light

the hidden sun, who messages the dawn,
sings a song that stirs the sleeping dove.
awakening geese call forth for the sun to lift.
a dance of dawning begins to play.
skirted girls, and a paper boy
wrapped in canvas cloth and a cardinals cap;
wave as they seek their destinations.
do you ever stand in the midst of such dance,
to wonder if your mother listens for geese?
does dawn still come to her beyond this place?
does she know that you come here most every morning
to beg thanks for breath? to remember; to forget?

more lines from a thank you note...

...thanks also for a worn wicker couch
for south seeing window panes that reveal the moon
thanks for the silent moon
and thanks for limbs and leaves seen through such shaded light
thanks for the need to sit here alone and silent
for the quietness of a dog
for resolution to at last begin my list
thanks for accepting imperfections
and thanks for quiet energy
now coming alive in my life
many thanks

To live along the bayou

I ask you to go with me to live along the bayou.
We will rent a small wood house made of shingle and stone
With space for wisteria and on occasion for pear
And be in solitude midst sparrows who sing.

We will learn there much love, learn love beyond ourselves
From sparrows singing, from sounds of geese; we will learn love
And remember grandmother songs to sing sometimes to children.
When evening comes we will listen.

Slow wings of longing impel me there;
I surrender to the call of sunlight at sundown; and silence;
Of red dogs who will race to us; of one ancient one who beckons.
I ask you to go with me to live along the bayou.

Ian

Have you seen ian, who tended to dogs?
No one has.
He lived down the rail embankment,
Inside an unkempt hedge.
Do you recall him?
He never cut his hair or went shaven
And washed himself from a kennel hose.
Last week he fought his cousin,
The one who makes whiskey.
The one who runs whiskey from Timberlake woods.
Another cousin now tends the dogs.

talk of aunt lelia

i walk the woods with daddy,
holding baskets of fallen figs;
gathered from the ground.
we compete with hummingbirds,
sometimes geese, for their sweetness.
also dad tells of aunt lelia,
taken to california
in a wood wagon pulled by horses.
she went with her father;
having grieved her mother,
in the year of nineteen nine.
we walk through a field of carved stone;
the name lelia is sometimes seen;
while geese ascend the northern sky
mysterious in their eternal path.
our path here turns quiet;
i no longer long for things far away;
but, maybe next year's figs;
another walk with dad.

along the road

she learned to celebrate each moment of sadness
her life of loss now brought
quiet stillness and surrender
to begin once more
to see life for the first time
bound in communion with spirit and mystery
bound in awkward energy
to manifest a strange beauty
to learn to dance

...thanks also

...thanks also for her gracious life
for songs sung in remembrance and celebration
by kin and friends returned to stand and weep and speak
to say the truth she became
thanks for sunlight down from a western sky
and for shadows from limb and leaf
for a wicker bed that became a place of prayer
for the memory of fourth grade teachers
thanks that life can be lived in imperfect exclusion
of electronic sound
many thanks

a cousin

we were fourteen when first i saw her face.
cousin lucy from mississippi;
who rode the greyhound bus to town,
in blue overalls fading to grey
and sandals seasoned by walks on sand.
shade from ancient trees made simple her steps
as she traveled to a place of protection;
our wooden house surrounded by porches.
her daddy had transferred to texas
while her mother sipped and slept throughout each day.
while with us, in clarinet, she grew proficient;
later, learned to lead the band;
even paraded on broadway and sang.
she never saw her dad again;
nor knew his other child.
when her mom died she did go home,
weeping beneath her fine straw hat.

lines from a thank you note...

...thanks also for a thin tanned lady;
and small girls who seek to ascend her garden's gate.
for a brown faced boy soon to travel alone
and red feathered birds along the fence
before they flee to their canopies of green.
thanks for roofs that ward away wind and rain
and for places to curl ourselves and dream
when weariness issues a command
to cease such complicated seeking.
thanks for seeking; for weariness.

again

in my dream
last night in my dream
i saw my brother
he has "reached the far side".
in dream though, as always,
he showed a precious smile;
as when he scores at par.
i felt recognized
and asked about his game;
he gently asked for mine.
then spoke his own.
"i play all day each day
in midst of all of you.
sometimes i laugh, sometimes i weep,
always i am with you."

My Song

Thank you for holding me
For displacing fright from deep within me
For putting to flight the causes for desperation

I do not understand this sense of beauty you bring me
And have no wish to know save gratitude

Even if I am in your midst always will I desire you
Always your loveliness will command my heart

I know my passion for you comes from beyond
Is it strange for me to think it divine

To the silence of my heart you come
Here now is your song ever lifting me

These eyes at last begin to see
For you now I can attend our garden
Can hold all children

My every aspect sings in delight

All of each part of me
Brings singing my love to you

Your brightness has become my being
Has become this land in which we live

How can I have arrived in this lovely place
Consumed by your kindness
All of me always sings softly to you

Driving from memphis

Kudzu claimed her roadside
Each fence and field and tree imprisoned
As also old barns enrapt in vine.

As a child I wondered
If tribes were lost there
Hidden beneath the green.

One time our bus became broken,
So we stood at an edge searching.
Beneath the green was washed away dirt.

We saw no tribes only goats
And always men in overalls;
Mules in leather harness;

Once we saw a seagull
Amidst northbound geese.

thinking back...

often, when she thinks back
and takes comfort to herself
for becoming a golden scout,
cheerleader captain
or member of the choir;
an edginess descends.
uncertain sadness comes.
she then recalls those times, when
as a stranger she awakened
so lost and alone.
not able to go to her home.
how did she ever return?

Jimmy

do you see him on cold mornings walking from the woods?
how he stumbles slowly; drifting behind the old trolley station;
where he remains for a while;
only to emerge, still disheveled but washed and in a sun dried shirt.
do you remember him before he went to war?
when he played for high school and made first team?
how in boys choir he sometimes sang solo?
how he always sat with his grandmother?
now he seems to never sing or clearly remember.
he can pronounce no words on war or where he has been.
firemen pull a chair for him beside the station door.
he sits alone and waves a stiff salute as people pass.
where is the boy he was? can any hear his song?
where are those who sent him to war? will they come here
to sit and wave and say what happened?
do you see him stiffly stand and return alone into the woods?

before you arrive

anticipations enfold me;
ceaseless murmurs always sing
inside my eager soul;
like an invisible choir
put there to energize each breath.
today
i no longer listen for earlene the dog
to bark the postman's arrival;
hoping for confirmation of acceptance in some club;
nor do i care if it snowed fourteen inches in omaha.
please have the moon tell me
your car is fifteen minutes north
of the blue and white cafe
scheduled to arrive here in sixty minutes.
i will fall on my knees in gratitude,
quiver until i hear your car door slam.

on a late winter night

while we breathe the first flow of arctic air,
ice embraces fallen leaves,
moonlight begins to fade.
the oak branches,
now as empty as rose stems appear,
while the light of morning begins.
there are no shadows.
i know sunshine soon shall reign,
will reassure each fig and ginkgo
to be of patience and surrender
toward that eternal moment
when energy comes again.
meanwhile, a man makes no sound,
pulls himself closer inside his coat
while he watches the silent street.
he cannot count his times standing there;
that he longed to go back inside.
how he got into his car;
begged trees for energy;
headed out from home.

a boy

on a bicycle, no longer abandoned;
like a stoop worker in the field,
a brown faced boy shines with perspiration
as he pedals, in immense circles, through the humid town.
and through an iron gate; 'Magnolia Cemetery' the sign said.
in curving circles grey stone surrounds the trees.
soft grasses lie on the graves and lawn.
it is the time of day when sparrows rest in patient shade
when mourners leave for luncheon or poignant memory;
when the tent is struck; when stooped men with shovels emerge;
when the paper grass is stripped away; when the coffin descends.
the boy, his bicycle again abandoned, emerges
and stands among the stooped, still perspiring.
his eyes glance widely at the men
then, already in retreat, looks into the grave.

not long after dark

he was standing on the porch
with bare back damp from perspiration
and his heart pumped so you could see his chest move.
he looked out through the trees
to his small bike
wheels spinning more slowly with each rotation
afraid to go there,
moonlight scarcely being enough.

west of Clarksdale

cypress trees stand where the river curls south,
they cast long shadows down the water.
insect songs fill each humid morning.
soft feathered egrets stand inside the shade.
sometimes they fly beyond the village
long abandoned and in flood floated south.
now and then an old man comes, to search
for his mother's yard, seeking what is lost.

sister's porch

i never can see its image
nor recall trees now towering there.
i do remember women, quietly speaking,
circled, on a screen porch, shucking corn.
there are few other sounds save wind;
sometimes aunt sissy singing;
sometimes a distant voice
calling children to come home.

more lines from a thank you note ...

... thanks again for breeze stirred ginkgo leaves
adrift in silence to the sunlit sidewalk;
and for a yellow lawn. for twin cousins
who come each year with great aunt lilly;
weighted down with pecan pie bread pudding;
with oysters mosca and peanut butter cake.
thanks for another day, for time to listen.
thanks for knowing to sit still and listen.
for baby sisters who look like dad
who looked like great grandmother.
thank you.

south into Mississippi

my face is in the rounded window
of a southbound greyhound bus.
i am ten.
four thin fingers and a thumb
hold close a leather bag
handed to me by dad.
he kissed me.
my mississippi travels began,
more or less in the custody of fanny emory,
a friend, also headed south;
we sit near the buses back,
behind the 'for colored' sign;
not far behind two on their way home soldiers
recruited by dad to further insure my safety.
past fields corn and cotton, beyond silos silver,
through pasture and forest filled with silent cows.
from beneath sackcloth scarves women stare;
sometimes they wave.
then the town with streets and houses.
out the round window i see her standing,
anxious almost but excited.
she receives me and my leather bag
in full embrace; and we walk home.

a love letter

you will notice in me, when i return,
a slowness in rising from the couch.
and my heart may beat so you can see it
when from the room i walk along the lawn.
i will not hire lee kilzoy and his band
nor expect to dance snowflakes from the street
or drink the bourbon flagons until dry
when pink shows first above the cypress trees.
i do desire to sleep so near to you
your rounded shoulders fit inside my arm,
and warmly feel your hip against my thigh,
to see strands of your hair moved by breathing;
to live such love, as now consumes my heart,
made more precious in these vanishing days.

In the low grasses

in low grasses we wait
sometimes touching in silence
then in deep anticipation continue
to beyond anticipation
who could ever dream of this
of quietness and laughter
each returning to sleep
amidst sunshine and afternoon

sometimes he waves

he walks the long lake road
not appropriately dressed
as in barefeet in winter or clown clothes
his lips move in constant speech
occasionally he quietly sings
we were friends from third grade
later he was sent to fight in vietnam
since then he walks the long lake road
sometimes he waves

a while ago from an early morning meditation

how can i channel you
i want all your breath
your stillness
your movement
to reside in me
please let your intimate breathing enshroud me
let aloneness transform all of me
let it become joy
let sadness become gentle strongness
become a garden of peace
teach me to call out to one who weeps
to invite him to sing
to awkwardly dance
teach me to sing
teach me to dance

Again

ice came to places out my window
on winds that have been in western missouri.
winds that began, mysterious as all things divine,
high above the western troposphere.
but who cares for the origin of cold?
so again, ice comes to the edge of all.
first as rain, held to leafless branches,
then, transformed to itself, imprisoning each branch,
to sublime, glistening, weightfulness..
what beauty the cold wind brings.

along the road

she learned to celebrate each moment of sadness
her life of loss now brought
quiet stillness and surrender
to begin once more
to see life for the first time
bound in communion with spirit and mystery
bound in awkward energy
to manifest a strange beauty
to learn to dance

Seasons

I recall when mom was four, her daddy died;
Grandmother and baby brother also survived.
In seasons, sometimes lonesome and bare,
Life became watching others pass by;
Standing in the schoolhouse window
Dreaming of the times when;
When there would be more than waiting.
Would sister Bessie soon come,
bring her car, stay for weeks?

In april

When redbud blooms appear
I never think that they might be owned
Who could own lovliness?

I drive a daughter's street
And dream to see grandsons
 racing beneath the trees

I cannot recall races
Beneath such purple beauty
But always I see the flowered trees

And I want to be beneath them
For april to become forever
But then flowers turn into leaves

Maybe I can stand in that shade
When the boys go to Wisconsin

A deep path

There is this deep path
It is my place to dwell
Along its way I dream
To be companions,
For us to forever dwell here
Step on step
Coming more to love;
To walk beside my love.

It is a sacred place.
One can be silent here
Its stillness is a refuge.

Here also I sing
To dance along the path.

inside

thank you for always seeking.

Always inside every aspect of me is you.
You are all I desire; you are my every hope.
My most beautiful certainty is your presence;
My every step is you within me.
You lift from me
Every aspect of being afraid
And allow me kindness and concern.
In morning you bring me the sun, its warmth against my face.
You are in the pale evening moon
All of energy emerges from your being.
You receive me again and again.
This is a truth outside all expression
And cannot be shouted or sung or written down.
It exists beyond all thought or dream or hope.
My life's reality is you.

Always inside every aspect of me is you.

I love to be here--

To have no space except this small place;
To search in winter the naked trees
Knowing not the origin of leaves.
Only that there is light here,
And I belong.

Come here

Here there is always laughter
Filled with love, gracious.
We can here yet see a curved moon.
I know you own sadness
And sadness walks these fields also.bur here we learn to walk sadness,
To become surrounded
simultaneously
by fields of green strongness
now near absent from frigid limitation
and flowers of laughter grown from surrender
flowers filled with gracious love.
Come my beloved
Live this love with me.

A note of explanation

Along the oak clad drive are roses
tended sometimes by great uncle Arthur.
Abandoned croquet wickets still stand
Amidst grown up lawn grasses.
Seldom sat in wooden chairs receive rain.

I want to leave here in a slow soft rain;
To not really understand the destination
But to be washed from here in never ending mist.

To stand in the damp and wave farewell;
To not know names written on my ticket;

To wash up among none who know me;
To have no idea how I was in fifth grade.

Taking two roses

I sit and breathe peace
My meditations manifest the dawn.
Then from unobserved places
The hideous demon dread descends
Spraying out its paralyzing poison
Consuming every moment
And making dead my desire to breathe
Making silent my hope
It was as if my enemy
Was an invisible phlegm like plastic
In total consumption of me.
This happened this morning.
I managed to stand and, in flight, walk outside
Not followed by consuming ooze
And I did not look back to further examine.
Instead I sat on the steps and embraced my dog
And then breathed all the way in
Breathed all my breath all the way out
I sat still in the remaining dawn
Deciding to simultaneously
Invite dread to join as I embraced

To breathe as I breathe;

To be consumed also by the dawn
By the beauty of daisies as they come to light;
By hummingbirds in their hesitations
To be healed as I am healed
By release to what causes kindness
And release of every aspect of perfection;
To depend on an energy
That causes birds to fly.
Then I stood and walked to roses,
Taking two, including stems.
I walk inside to make our coffee and vase the roses
To place the vase and one cup
Beside my beloved.

On awakening

A brown rose pulled in gleaning;
Food on simple plates, red floor tile end on end.
A boy and a dog enter from the garden,
The boy laden with tomatoes and watermelon
Sits beside his dog.
They clean their plates.
Backs to a fenced yard they move.
The boy walks on to school
While the dog lays, nose touching the glass door.
The gleaner sips coffee from her cup
Standing there in stillness.
She is delighted that dove provide the only sound;
Then I come from the porch;
She allows such return

again

more lines from a thank you note.....

...thanks also for moments of silence;
for recollection of egrets soaring south
beneath reflections of the october moon.
thanks for the smell of baking cookies;
for time taken as they became baked.
for every moment as children arrive.
thanks for a friend who weaves such cloth
as embraces our back and shoulders.
thanks for the white haired one who waves hello;
for the little girl who plays on the sidewalk.
thank you

an emigrant

a young emigrant
whose passage brought indenture
years bent in labor
who gave her precious grandson
to fight for independence
sleeps beneath a stone
committed to her sacred honor
from within that place
a spirit of freedom flows
'open your arms let them in'

to be in fields

i also dream to walk in valley fields;
along thin dirt roads beyond villages.
away from work and from anxious voices.
to sit on abandoned wood wagon seats
and see not one person; or maybe one
who walks, cane in hand, to the river's side.
i dream to be silent among small birds;
among wild roses entwined by forest.
to embrace energy from inside them.

dancing with the moon

enroll soon in blue moon's school for dancing
name a reason to stand among those glancing
rolling eyes up to the skies; hesitate
outside yourself; with joy anticipate
leaps stratospheric! Receive moon's reply,
leap onto the floor, dance until you fly!

At evening

We walk amid our roses at day's end,
The streets are unlit; walker's pass and wave
This day's work is done, dishes washed and stacked
Rose stems no longer loosened from lattice
Sister's images painted on the fence
Gaze out to us
We with thanks recall
The days she drew them and wish forever
Her quiet return
A moon now appears
So we in silence wait and remember
Betina the cat who comes to be playful
Settles soon for embrace and then for sleep
We also seek for sleep and stand to return.
Our places of rest await
Ever they call

Except for song

she continues to sing
even as the children sleep
she stands near a back porch door
an asleep baby held to her breast
silent except for song
i want a job like that
singing songs to children and myself
sometimes even stopping for a nap

again

do not have concern
you hoarders of soft blue socks
my feet love naked
today is like spring
children swarm half empty streets
who cares if it rains
snow becomes water
sisters weep for melted men
a waste truck arrives
my dog spends her life
nose pressed to the front window
moaning for a cat
shrill tornado bells
sing each thursday afternoon
only rehearsal

Sam

listen to me now
at dawn i saw a small red fox
sound asleep on sammy's grave
why would i become filled with envy
i stood there
then wept to take rest there
to awaken and be beautiful
again with sam walk around the hill

Here

Many thanks
For dirt paths that disappear from the road.
Thanks for uncut forest land
And for every mite and stallion abiding there;
For steepness in hills and fields beyond where trees can grow
For flat rock to lay upon beneath sun and moon
And circle of stars inside the black night
Configured outside all imagination
Unchanged ever by the issues of man.
Thanks for the touch of bare feet against dirt
A hand to shield sunshine from my eye
For the feel of sun against my cheek
Thanks for a place to be even if in dream
Untouched by pavement and electronic signal
Thanks for geese in northern flight
For sight to see them
For breath
Thanks

Your light

I began so empty
Then was filled by disturbed circumstance
Always to seek true romance
Or equal sad history.

From emtiness I wept
Then through each broken down place
You swept these wounds out to a space
Beyond sweet promises kept

You shined light into me
And sent your energy
So now I am delighted to sing
To dance with you and sing

Breath and life
a poem of thanks

many thanks to you for breath and life
for sleep
and for the touch of love against my skin
for shadow and light
an emergent rose
sparrows
freedom to turn away from frightful strife
for occasions difficult and beyond all ken
and the means to walk as the path narrows.
all thanks for friends faithful and strange
children, cousins, sweet sisters and beyond
for dogs
for one who makes laughter
and prays
for you whose beauty will not be explained.
thanks.

for john lennon's song 'imagine'
and george's 'my sweet lord' or 'come to san francisco'.
or hearing 'skips of fandango' once again.
thanks for memory of men named lomax.
thanks for desperation and for prayer;
for energy as flows from such circumstance;
for rhythms that flow as we listen;
and songs we sing to one another.
thanks for brother fred gone to sing and dance
in another room; in another room.
thank you.
much love.

more lines from a thank you note.....

... thanks for soft spread leaves that cover her tomb.
thanks also for the scent of a flowered dress
flat ironed and smooth
worn always for my arrival;
for her endurance of widowhood
from the age of twenty six
for her
still remembered songs sung again and again.
for surety of being loved.
thanks for always knowing i could arrive,
and walk the wooded grove hand in hand.
for being taught 'mr froggy went a courting'.
many thanks

Loss

please listen to me
i saw sister's pasture shed burn.
inside were brother bert's clothes.
including his eagle scout medals
my heart aches
maybe, if next we meet,
he will recognize how dark smoke
clouded across the mississippi.

Dream recollection

early
at daylight
I walked outside to breathe
To wander the field
Waving farewell to stars
As if we might never meet again.
I lay down in the short grass
As light slowly ascends
Coming into union
With the greened field.
My eyes closed,
In that moment a dream resumed
Children sing to me from a hidden place
Their voices together
Mystically call to me.
Awaken they sing, awaken
Not from this moment
Awaken to sing with us;
To never leave this field.
So I decided to stay and sing
My ankles surrounded by grass

Spirit of love

Inside these instinctive walls
We arrive without fear, without wiseness,
Clasped by terminal lonesomeness,
Desperate for energy
To be beyond such confinement.

Then love spirit always comes
Eager to enter, to be within;
To become with us as one,
Our manifestor of kindness,
Of ecstasy, of embrace,
Of endurance and courage--
The transformer of all things lonesome.

In this decisive moment
Desperation is our friend
We surrender what we are
And can ever become
We infuse with courage
We unite with spirit
To become what love will have us be
To be beyond confinement

In the land of lelia

Coldwater cemetery road still twists
Beneath oceans of yesterday's snow
Imprisoned in ice-bent trees
While its flagpole lays, asunder and fallen,
Partially wrapped in frozen flags.

As a boy I could never not flee this road
Or flee from aunt lelia
When she sat among the tombs
Telling me of her daddy, christopher columbus brown,
 wounded in battle at shiloh.

The songs of lelia often return
Years since we sat there
I hear her fallen father moan
Seventeen years old, bloodily wounded,
His body broken, he lay still in sure defeat.

The coldwater road is now covered by concrete
With a dividing line and left turn lanes
An automobile plant covers the space
Once covered by lelia's farm

Author Scheduling,
Book Sales and Contact Information

Billy Reed is a skillful wordsmith and eloquent conversationalist. Consider inviting Billy Reed to give a reading at your next social gathering. For additional copies of this book, or to schedule a reading and book-signing, please contact the author at the links provided below.

Website: http://billyreedpoetry.com/
Book: https://www.createspace.com/6970826
E-Mail: bill@wlreed.com